This Awesome Coloring Book
Belongs To

I
AM
AWE
SOME

GIRLS
ARE
COOL

I AM
Beautiful

Make
Today
Magical

I am
Very
Brave

I Am
Creative

Good
Vibes
Only

YES
GIRL
YOU
CAN

If I Can
Dream it
I Can
Do it

YOU
TOTALLY
GOT
THIS

CHOOSE
HAPPY

Breathe
in
Breathe
Out

Don't Worry Be Happy

Relax

I Have
Many
Talents
and
Gifts

THINK
HAPPY
BE
HAPPY

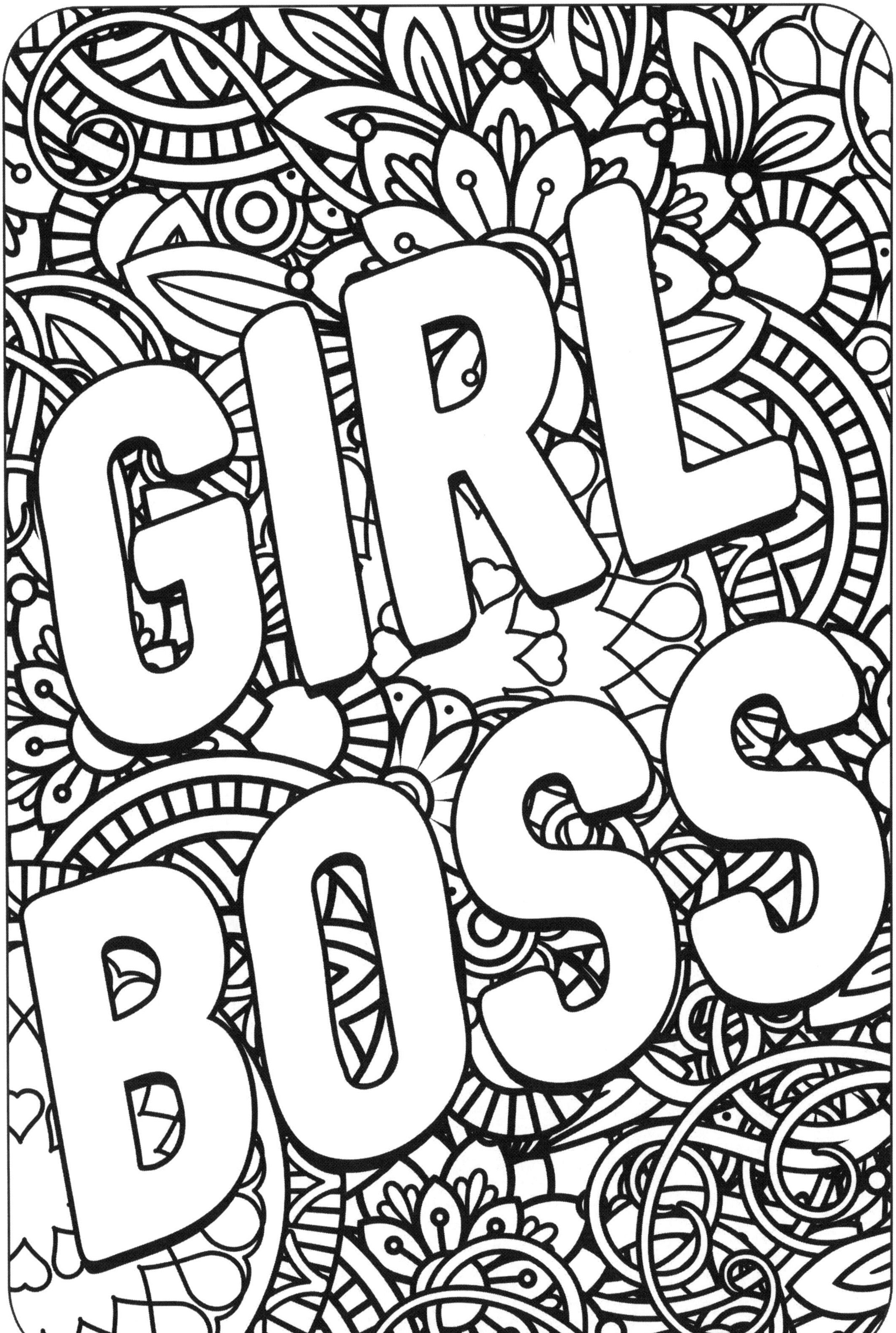
GIRL
BOSS

ENJOY
EVERY
MOMENT

I CAN
DO
AMAZING
THINGS

Think
Happy
Thoughts

Color
Testing
Page

Made in the USA
Coppell, TX
18 December 2022

90225401R00026